Let's Go!

Train Rides

By Pamela Walker

Children's Press
A Division of Grolier Publishing
New York / London / Hong Kong / Sydney
Danbury, Connecticut

Photo Credits: Cover, pp. 5, 7, 9, 13, 15, 17, 21 by Thaddeus Harden; pp. 11, 19 © Index Stock

Contributing Editors: Mark Beyer and Eliza Berkowitz
Book Design: MaryJane Wojciechowski

Visit Children's Press on the Internet at:
http://publishing.grolier.com

Cataloging-in-Publication Data

Walker, Pamela
   Train rides / by Pamela Walker.
     p. cm. — (Let's go!)
   Includes bibliographical references and index.
   Summary: Simple text and photographs describe a train
 ride, including the work of the engineer and the conductor.
   ISBN 0-516-23104-9 (lib. bdg.) — ISBN 0-516-23029-8 (pbk.)
   1. Railroad travel—Juvenile literature 2. Railroads—Trains—Juvenile literature
   [1. Railroads—trains] I. Title II. Series.
   2000
 385—dc21

Contents

I am going on a train ride.

Other people are going on the train with us.

5

I sit down when I ride the train.

There are a lot of seats on a train.

I like to sit near the window.

I give my **ticket** to the **conductor**.

The conductor punches a hole in the ticket.

The ticket can be used only once.

9

Trains ride on long **tracks**.

Many trains go over bridges.

Hillsmere Elementary
Media Center

11

I like to look out the window when I ride on a train.

I see another train going the other way.

13

This is the **control room**.

The **engineer** sits in the control room.

The engineer drives the train.

15

The engineer pushes a button.

The button blows the horn.

17

Trains also go through tunnels.

Tunnels are dark, but trains have big, bright lights.

66.90

19

Now the train stops at the **station**.

We get off the train.

We are here!

21

New Words

conductor (kun-**duk**-tor) person who takes tickets on a train

control room (kun-**trol room**) place where engineer sits to run a train

engineer (en-jih-**neer**) person who runs a train

station (**stay**-shun) place where trains stop to pick up people and drop them off

ticket (**tih**-kut) paper slip that lets you take a train ride

tracks (**traks**) rails on which trains ride

To Find Out More

Books

The Big Book of Trains
by Christine Heap
DK Publishing

Trains
by Gallimard Jeunesse
and James Prunier
Scholastic, Incorporated

Trains: A True Book
by Darlene R. Stille
Children's Press

Web Site
U.S. Railroad Retirement Board
http://www.rrb.gov/teachers.html
Check out this site to learn more about trains!

Index

About the Author
Pamela Walker lives in Brooklyn, New York. She takes a train to work every day, but enjoys all forms of transportation.

Reading Consultants
Kris Flynn, Coordinator, Small School District Literacy, The San Diego County Office of Education

Shelly Forys, Certified Reading Recovery Specialist, W.J. Zahnow Elementary School, Waterloo, IL

Peggy McNamara, Professor, Bank Street College of Education, Reading and Literacy Program